Cl

CW00968291

UK

**By Anne
Sparrowhawk**

Cartoons:
Phil Hailstone

Published by:

Teachers' Pocketbooks
Laurel House, Station Approach,
Alresford, Hampshire SO24 9JH, UK
Tel: +44 (0)1962 735573
Fax: +44 (0)1962 733637
E-mail: sales@teacherspocketbooks.co.uk
Website: www.teacherspocketbooks.co.uk

*Teachers' Pocketbooks is an imprint of
Management Pocketbooks Ltd.*

Series Consultant: **Brin Best**.

© Anne Sparrowhawk.

This edition published 2004.

ISBN 1 903776 55 4

British Library Cataloguing-in-Publication
Data – A catalogue record for this book is
available from the British Library.

Design, typesetting and graphics by Efex Ltd.
Printed in UK.

Contents

Author Acknowledgements

This book is based on experiences I have enjoyed as a governor of Cottenham Primary School, and on work with many content creators and software developers. Most of all it has a firm grounding in practical activities with children and teachers in classrooms throughout the country. Many of the teachers I have had the privilege of observing and talking with do not fully appreciate how creative and skilful they are in managing a complex cocktail of environment, materials, resources and people. I would like to extend my gratitude to my colleagues at Sparrowhawk and Heald Ltd, who stimulate my thinking, and in particular to Jamie Stanfield who worked with me on the first draft.

Introduction

 ICT Equipment

 Choosing & Using Software

 ICT for Class Teaching

 ICT for Learning

 The Internet

 ICT at Home

 Inclusion

Introduction

How to use this pocketbook

There are no magic answers to using ICT effectively in the classroom.
Confidence in your own use of ICT and a knowledge of the different types of
resources available and how best to use them certainly help!

This book tries to give hints and tips about some of the resources available and ways
of using them based on the experiences I have had in visiting many classrooms in
primary and secondary schools throughout the UK. One of the biggest challenges
facing education is how to share good practice effectively. Some of these pages offer
simple checklists, others indicate factors that you might want to take into account
when planning ICT. All of them can be personalised to match your situation and
context.

What is Information Communication Technology (ICT)?

When we talk about ICT these days we are usually referring to a new piece of computer-related equipment. *Digital, web, email, interactive* are all terms that relate directly to the computer's part in ICT.

However, much more falls under the heading than PC or internet-related equipment. Typical ICT equipment for the following age groups would be:

3-5 year olds	5+ year olds
Audio entertainment – cassette tapes	Computers (including laptops and
TV, video, CD, DVD	Personal Digital Assistants [PDAs])
Remote control toys	Digital TV
Calculators	Games consoles
Digital cameras	Internet-enabled mobile phones
Games consoles	Digital cameras
Telephones	Data-logging equipment – sensors and probes
Computers, software	Film editing equipment

We can **communicate** through it, **interact** with it or **store** data upon it.

What is special about ICT?

Whilst cynics will say, *'Humans make mistakes, but to really foul up you need a computer,'* computers do have some really powerful features.

- **Storage** – A small computer can hold more information than would fill a four-drawer filing cabinet – and you can **search** it too!
- **Repeatability** – Computers can apply the same **process** to a range of data and take almost instant account of changing factors.
- **Changing data** – Drafting work and amending it, editing last month's agenda or re-using the format of the notes is easy using **stored** data.
- **Sharing information** – ICT provides the power to **share** documents, planning information, data, images, or any digital resource with colleagues either in school or across the country.
- **Presentation skills** – Formatting work so that it looks professional is important to teachers as well as children, and ICT allows standards to be agreed and maintained.

What is special about ICT?

ICT is not just a **subject** – it is also a set of skills that everyone needs in the modern world. With everything from our televisions to shop tills becoming ever more complex, these skills will be necessary no matter what your students want to do.

Use ICT tools when it suits you; don't feel you have to incorporate them for their own sake. Think of other professions and how they use technology. A good calculator doesn't make a good accountant any more than a digital projector makes a good teacher, yet they will both greatly assist people who use them correctly.

Great lesson plan + ICT =   Great ICT + poor lesson plan = ✗

Teaching specific ICT skills will ensure that children have the tools they need to continue their learning. But you cannot learn to use a word-processor without using words, or a spreadsheet without using numbers. The best ICT courses teach students to use ICT in a **context**. Understanding **when** and **how** to use ICT is just as important as knowing how to operate it.

Hardware, software and peripherals

Hardware is the stuff that you can touch – your monitor, keyboard, processor and mouse. Often bought as a single unit, these items, designed to work together, make up a computer.

Software includes the programs that allow you to type, draw, or surf the internet. You can't touch software, but you can get it to do things by moving your mouse or typing. Software has usually been written for a specific sort of computer – PC or Apple for example – with a certain amount of memory.

Peripherals include printers, whiteboards and scanners, and are designed to work with computers with certain features, so check that they will work with **your** computers.

Hardware	Software	Peripherals
Modem	Word processors	Printer
Mouse	Spreadsheets	Interactive whiteboard
Keyboard	Databases	Scanner
Monitor	Games	Data-logger
CD-ROM drive	Animations	
	Operating system	

The scope of ICT use in schools today

Few schools can boast that they have anywhere near the ICT resources they need, yet a recent report showed that 88% of teachers use computers regularly to teach. *(DfES Survey of Information and Communications Technology in Schools, 2002)*

ICT is used:

- Across all subjects, ages, and in and out of the curriculum
- To increase the amount of access students have to learning tools
- To support students in their own self-directed learning
- To facilitate whole-class teaching
- To give students access to learning outside normal school lessons and hours
- To foster the ICT skills necessary for students to engage fully in modern society

Different models of ICT implementation

There are many different models of computer implementation in schools.
These are usually determined by a combination of circumstances – budget, school
architecture, staff skills and interests, school management strategy.

Whatever the model offered in your school, the issues that affect its success are likely
to be:

- Staff (**all staff**) skills and familiarity with ICT for their own use
- Opportunities for students to access ICT
- Availability of resources in
  lesson time and out of
  school hours
- Reliability of resources
- Technician availability
- Degree to which ICT is
  embedded into the
  school curriculum

Different models of ICT implementation

Computer suite

Suites enable whole classes of children to learn and practise particular ICT skills. In primary schools **suites** usually have 15 computers, so students often have to share a computer throughout a lesson. In secondary schools suites are often subject related, so the ICT department has a suite, and maybe science and maths too.

Key issues for effective use of ICT suites:

- Are there enough computers for one per child or do the children share?
- Working in pairs at a computer can be very effective – do children go into the suite expecting a machine each?
- How much time does each child have in the suite per week?
- Is there space around the computer for children to write or follow a worksheet?
- Where can children save their work? Can they then access that work from computers elsewhere in the school?
- Does the layout allow you to teach the whole class and see all the students?
- Does the suite support independent learning by displaying instructions about common tasks?

Different models of ICT implementation

Cluster of computers in the classroom

Clusters can be very effective in primary schools or in specialist classrooms in secondary schools. Space is an issue and often limits what can be achieved.

Where clusters of computers are used as part of a daily carousel of activities, sheets on the wall nearby can:

- Provide general instructions for computer use, such as:
    - Instructions for saving work
    - Information about how to carry out searches on the internet or in reference works
- Provide specific task instructions
- Manage the list of students working on the computer
- Provide a record of work completed

Different models of ICT implementation

Teacher computer as a resource

Many teachers now have their own computer. This has increased teacher skill and confidence significantly.

Common uses	Issues to consider
Lesson planning	Is your PC compatible with the school system?
Creating worksheets	Do you have a licence to use school software?
Creating presentations for use in class	What is the best way of sharing information between your own PC and the school?
Researching	If you need to have internet access regularly, can and should you upgrade your internet access at home?
Emailing	Should you have your own email address specifically for school-related activities?
Mid-term and long-term planning	Back-ups – where and how can you store these?
Reporting – to parents/carers and colleagues	If you are taking a laptop to and from school, what are the insurance implications?
School admin – agendas etc.	Should you allow your own family access to your computer? Might there be confidential information that they should not access?

Different models of ICT implementation

Computers in the library

Computers in the library are valuable as an extension of the paper-based reference resources held there. There are some implications for use that need to be addressed.

Practical issues	Issues to consider
How many computers?	If study skills form part of the curriculum, are there enough computers to facilitate this in the library space?
Is the internet available?	If the internet is available, are there filters that ensure students do not access inappropriate materials?
How much supervision is possible?	Are library staff able to support students using the computers?
Can students save their work to the network?	If the resources are used for students' research, can they save to a network location that they can access elsewhere?
Are CD-ROMs available? How are they stored and presented? Do they have to be installed before use?	Supporting CD-ROMs through a CD-ROM sharer can enable a large number of CD-ROMs to be installed and made available for communal access.
Who manages subscriptions to internet sites?	Librarians are often responsible for magazine subscriptions. How should internet subscriptions be purchased in school?

ICT Equipment

Laptop computers

Weighing less than 2kg, today's **laptops** are virtually indistinguishable from desktop computers in terms of processing power and facilities. They do enable and encourage a different kind of use, though:

Class use	Issues
A flexible alternative to ICT suite teaching. Particularly valuable in relation to science experiments, for example.	Puts ICT in supportive classroom role. Needs to be managed carefully for reliability.
More flexible classroom arrangement. All can face the front of the class and still use their laptop.	Leaves the teacher still at the front and directing the class.
Stored on a specially designed trolley, all classrooms can have equal access.	Must be disciplined in returning the laptops to charging trolley.
Wireless networks offer wire-free access to the school network and the internet.	Allows distributed access to the network and internet.
Students are likely to feel comfortable using ICT in their own classroom near their own desk; the technology comes to them.	Keeps the students in charge of their learning.

Desktop computers

The majority of computers older students will come into contact with will be **desktops**. Although top of the range laptops offer the same facilities as desktops, desktops still tend, on average, to have more memory. They have a number of advantages over laptops:

- Generally **more robust**
- Larger, **better quality monitors** for viewing animations or video clips
- **Better sound** resources
- **More memory** means that they can be used for more demanding applications, such as art packages or interfacing with music equipment

- May have a **faster graphics card** enabling them to present information on the screen very quickly. This is important for games software where the screen image is constantly changing
- Permanent location means **more care** can be taken over the seating, monitor angle and height of the desk or table than for portable computer use

Networked computers

The **server** is a shared computer space. All the computers connected to it can share the space. If you store files or data on the network server, any other computer with access to it can see it. Certain areas of this network can be closed off from students and maintained as an area strictly for teachers. Wireless Local Area Networks (WLANs) do this without cables, using a transmitter and using radio frequencies.

Benefits for teachers	Benefits for students
Resources for lessons can be stored on the network and opened or printed off from any computer the teacher chooses.	Allows students access to a range of cross-curricular material quickly and conveniently.
Teachers load resources once which all students can then open from the network.	Students feel empowered and included by saving work on to the shared network.
Teachers can leave extra course material on the network for students to look at when they please.	Students can access the lesson materials independently.
Central back-ups can be arranged so that the system becomes easier to manage.	Students don't have to remember or keep safe a floppy disk with their work on it.
The server can operate a virus check so that viruses do not infect the school system.	Fewer viruses will be introduced into the system.

Points to consider

Locating ICT equipment
Choosing where you site computers can have a very significant effect on how they are used. If you have a suite of 30 computers, students will assume they can have a computer each, though you may not always want that to be the case.

Pedagogical issues
Balance between ICT for whole class teaching and individual access to computers. Balance between focused ICT subject teaching and use of ICT across the curriculum.

Portable vs stationary
Whiteboards, digital projectors, and TVs can be moved from one location to another. Do you move the students to the resources or the resources to the students?

Available usage vs best usage
This is ultimately decided by your school's budget. Ideally, ICT resources would be placed within appropriate reach of students all the time. However, an interactive whiteboard in every classroom does not guarantee great ICT teaching and learning. The most important objective is **appropriate use of ICT**.

Other ICT equipment

Although we tend to think of ICT equipment in terms of computers and software, your school may have other ICT resources that you can use in conjunction with these.

Good practice in choosing hardware:

- Think about the **age** of the children and their **dexterity** and understanding
- Consider the **robustness** of the item
- Decide on the **top five features** you need the device to have
- Check **compatibility** with other equipment
- Read **reviews** in magazines and journals
- **Listen** to experiences of other teachers

Scanners

What use can you make of a scanner?

- Scanning images to include in students' work
- Scanning pages of students' work to act as evidence of learning outcomes
- Scanning documents to turn them into files that you can save electronically

Most scanners these days are 'flat-bed'. You place the picture/text or page face down and the scanner digitises it, saving it as a .tif file if you want to be able to manipulate the image and use it at a variety of sizes. If you want to use the image within a document, you may want to save it as a .jpg, and if you want to publish it on the web, as a .gif. These different file formats take up progressively less memory suiting them to their different purposes.

Alternatively, a scanner can be used as an **Optical Character Reader**, scanning in a written document and then, using special software, turning it into a text file that you can edit. The success of this process depends on the clean nature of the type and the sophistication of the character reading software.

Floor turtles

LOGO is a programming language through which children can learn to explore the ideas of a single command, a sequence of commands, and a procedure or short computer program. It was developed for the computer screen, but for young children it is easier to explore these ideas using a physical object, and the floor turtle enables just that.

- Commands can be given singly – FORWARD 100 and the turtle moves forward 100 units
- The turtle can be made to turn – RIGHT 90 or any other degree measurement
- The turtle can mark its route using a pen on the paper-covered floor
- Turtles are usually used at key stage 1 where the subject is introduced

By using a floor turtle children learn to plan, to think ahead, to hypothesise and, above all, to explain and describe the process to each other.

Digital imaging

Taking digital photographs has become standard practice in many families today. Digital photography can have a significant impact within schools too, but you need to consider a number of issues to make sure you choose the right camera.

What the digital camera might be used for	Implications
High quality art work/graphic	Needs high resolution – three megapixels or more.
Recording school trips for writing up later	Choose removable memory so that you can potentially take lots of pictures.
Creating a visual record of a student's work	Needs high resolution so that you can read texts.

Digital imaging

Camera users	Implications
Age of children using it	The sophistication of the user is important! If they are very young, then the quality of the image is probably not as important as the robustness of the camera.
Teachers' intentions	Make sure you know what they all hope to do.

Camera images	Implications
Could be transferred to the computer to be used in stories/presentations	Who will be responsible, and where will this happen?
Could be printed	Do you have a good high-quality printer? You may need to limit how many images children print.
Could be edited	Make sure you have suitable image editing software.

Digital video cameras

A digital video camera can provide evidence of activity or events to support children's evaluations of their own performance and others'. The choice is either a simple purchase of a basic consumer camcorder, or a much more specialised and expensive purchase. This table might help you decide:

Educational purpose	High quality video needed?	Editing output essential?	Child use essential?
Recording a musical/dramatic performance	✗	✗	✗
Recording a dance, or particular sequence or move in a sporting context	✗	✗	✓
To create the raw material for a film for drama, film studies or media studies	✓	✓	✓
To create a multimedia presentation	✓	✓	✓

Interactive whiteboards

An **interactive whiteboard** is a touch sensitive board on to which the image the computer displays is projected. When you touch the board you can control the computer directly.

Main benefits
- Exciting whole-class teaching using graphics, video, animation and sometimes sound
- Students as well as teachers can interact on a shared space
- Lessons can maintain pace through a variety of media and resources
- Everyone can see what is going on
- Enables editing on screen
- Can instantly 'flip back' to previous screens
- Can save work done on the whiteboard for next lesson or next term
- Motivating for both students and teachers!

Issues
- Permanent or mobile? What software comes with the board?
- Where is the projector placed?
- Cost of buying several for a school

Data projectors

A **data projector** connects directly to a computer and then projects the computer screen image on to a board or wall.

Main benefits

- Exciting whole-class teaching using graphics, video, animation and sometimes sound
- Lessons can maintain pace through a variety of media and resources
- Everyone can see what is going on
- Less expensive than an interactive whiteboard
- Motivating for both students and teachers!

Issues

- Has to be operated from the computer, so teaching is not necessarily at the board
- Cannot record any student or teacher actions on the materials presented

Data-logging equipment

A **data-logger** is a sensor that measures temperature, light, or sound, and is especially useful in measuring variables that change with time. It will show how long it takes for a cup of coffee to cool down, or an ice cube to melt, for example.

Mostly used in science, this resource works best to:

- Collect continuous data
- Collect quantitative data
- Collect multiple readings over time
- Present results visually, so students can see trends and patterns
- Present results as graphs, so time can be spent on analysis

Some logging devices have to be directly connected to the computer, while others can be remote and then download their data. The type of experiment you wish to carry out will determine which suits your needs.

Control equipment

Control equipment outputs to bulbs, buzzers and motors, using switches and sensors as inputs. The control box lets you enter a series of instructions to be carried out in sequence – this forms the program. A model of a lighthouse might have a program to switch on the light, wait 10 seconds, switch the light off, wait 5 seconds and switch the light on again. This could be achieved using control technology linked to a computer.

A checklist for purchase:

- Are you looking for a computer simulation of control or a device that will control external equipment?
- Does the program meet the needs of the curriculum?
- Is the program appropriately designed for the age group you are working with?
- Do you understand the full list of items you need to buy?
- Are you sure that the resources will work with your computer? Have you checked the interface they demand?
- Are the devices mains or battery powered?

Video conferencing resources

Video conferencing describes a process that can link people in different parts of the country or world. It has considerable potential for education, and has been discussed, for instance, as a mechanism for linking a group of disparate students to one teacher.

There are a number of practical issues involved, eg where the camera sits at each end of the conference and how much it is manipulated by an operative. While using video conferencing you can link:

- One person to another – each has a small camera located on top of the computer and can see a picture of themselves and their correspondent on screen
- One person to a group – a more typical teaching or lecturing scenario
- One group to another group
- A number of groups to each other – an option which requires a lot of equipment

The best way to find out about this technology at the moment is to explore it through a centre or university which has high quality resources. This kind of technology will be commonplace one day, but is not available to all just yet.

Websites

Advice on the best purchases needs to be **current**. Where possible seek advice related specifically to use in schools, and to real classroom practice. The organisations below have helpful websites.

Becta **www.ictadvice.org.uk**
Government agency with advice on ICT

Curriculum Online **www.curriculumonline.gov.uk**
Government-run website which lists software

National Curriculum Online **www.nc.uk.net**
Links every National Curriculum programme of study requirement to resources

NAACE **www.naace.org**
Organisation for advisors on the use of ICT in the classroom

TEEM **www.teem.org.uk**
Classroom-based evaluations of software from UK teachers

IPAS **www.ipas.ngfl.gov.uk**
Independent ICT procurement advisory service

Technical support

The role of **technical support** is critical in maintaining a working network or set of machines. The role should be balanced between planned activity and shorter term 'fire-fighting'. Use this checklist to decide where your school's technical support is going.

	Sometimes	Often	Always
Replacing printer cartridges			
Fixing computers that have crashed			
Setting up the digital projector			
Liaising with the telephone company			
Connecting peripherals			
Installing new software			
Cabling			
Setting up new machines			

Making the most of your budget

Hardware

Decide what you need	**Specify** your hardware requirements. Maximise your order by buying once a year, if you can, to get the best price. You need to balance that, though, with the workload of integrating the hardware all at once.
Decide how to buy	**Lease or purchase?** Do you need to write a **tender** or can you ask for **quotes?** Can the LEA help you with this?
Contact suppliers	**Local** firms might be interested, or larger **national companies**. Beware of shops that simply 'ship boxes'. They might have a good price, but poor follow-up and service.
Evaluate quotes/bids	Make sure you know what you are looking for in the quotes and try to **compare** like with like.
Place an order	Make sure that the **conditions of the order** are clear – if dates are important ensure the supplier has understood them in the quote.
Work with suppliers	Make sure that there are **staff available** to answer queries when the installation is happening.

Making the most of your budget

Software

Many educational publishers will allow you to install software on your home computer for your own use in lesson planning and preparation. When purchasing software **read the licence agreement** and **buy** only enough licences to suit your needs:

- **Network licence** means that all computers linked together on your school site can use a piece of software. If you have two separate networks within your school you will need two separate licences.
- **Site licence** means you can use the software on all the computers in your school, regardless of whether they are all linked together or not.
- Some licences limit you to the **number of computers** that can use the software **at a time**.
- Some licences limit you to the number of computers on which the software can be **installed**.
- **Standalone licence** usually means just that – a licence for one computer by itself.

Making the most of your budget

How much software do you need? Use this chart to help you think about how many licences you need for different types of software in your school.

Software type	All computers (Network or site licence)	Some computers (Network licence or licence for a specific number of computers)	One or two computers (Standalone maybe?)
Tools – word-processor, spreadsheet, database	✓	✗	✗
Art packages	✗	✓	✓
Dictionaries / encyclopaedias	✓	✓	✗
Subject specific programs – teaching maths, literacy, history, science for example	?	✓	✓
Assessment packages	✓	?	✗
Resources for SEN students	?	✓	✓
Resources for a particular year group	?	✓	✓

Making the most of your budget

Maintenance budget

Sometimes called the Total Cost of Ownership, maintenance should include the cost of installation of computers and network infrastructure, internet access, technical support and staff training.

The scale of these budget figures will be in direct relation to the number of computers owned and styles of usage, the frequency of printing out of children's work, for instance.

The maintenance budget will include:

Consumables
Cartridges and toner for printers
Paper for printers
Discs – floppy or writeable CD-ROMs
Memory for digital cameras
Batteries

Hardware that breaks easily
Mice
Keyboards
Headphones
Graphics Tablets
Spare Cables

Making the most of your budget

Maintenance Budget

This graphic might reflect some of the patterns of expense in your school. For example, there may be a high cost of consumables in the spring term when all the secondary students are completing and, therefore, printing out coursework. There could be a higher spend on hardware in the summer when some staff might have more time to fit the new equipment because Year 11 students have left, or other years are on activity week.

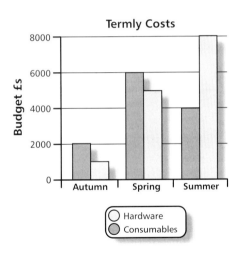

Making the most of your budget

Development budget

Sometimes it's a good idea to try out something new on a small scale before you equip the whole school. Buy a standalone piece of software and run it for a while, or, if you have more money to play with, one laptop or digital projector, or even a whiteboard.

When you are planning to try something new, whether a new type of computer, peripheral or software solution, it's a wise move in the long run to buy it and run it **somewhere where it will not interfere** with your working network.

And buying new equipment is good for staff morale – playing with new toys will motivate someone in your teaching team!

Introduction

 ICT Equipment

 Choosing & Using Software

 ICT for Class Teaching

 ICT for Learning

 The Internet

 ICT at Home

 Inclusion

Choosing & Using Software

Choosing software

Remember there are hundreds of pieces of software out there vying for your attention. Here are some tips to help you get the best for your money and your classroom:

- Is the title **relevant** to the National Curriculum?
- If it needs to be, is it **up-to-date**?
- Does its design enable children to use it with the minimum of **teacher intervention**?
- Does it offer **learning opportunities** that other media do not?
- Ask to **trial** any software that you are considering buying
- Look for an independent software **evaluation** on the TEEM website www.teem.org.uk

Content-rich software for the classroom

Content-rich software should offer:

- Text and pictures or diagrams at an **appropriate level** for your students
- **Enough information** to support the topic you are teaching
- Animations, simulations or video clips that **explain and illuminate** information
- Indexing and searching that **support students** identifying specific information
- Easy routes for children to **find their way** around
- Activities pitched at an **appropriate level**, or meaningfully differentiated to support your class's varying needs
- The opportunity to **extract small elements** of the resource for the students' own use. Beware of software that requires you to copy out screens and screens of information at once

Reference software

Reference software consists of more general reference materials to be used across the curriculum, eg dictionaries, encyclopaedias, atlases and newspapers.

The benefits of using a computer-based version of these should be:

- They are **up-to-date**
- They support a wide range of **search** possibilities
- You can use them **alongside** other pieces of software

Talk to other teachers to find out what resources are available in other parts of the school, what you could group together to purchase and what is available freely on the internet.

Software for PSHE and citizenship

Software to support these subjects may be different in nature from the
information-rich software that other subjects require. It can present:

- Scenarios that students **recognise** and so reassure them that it is OK to
  discuss such situations
- **Objective** information – on bullying or insecurity, for instance
- Different people's **perspectives** on a particular situation
- **Stimuli** for discussion without relying on personal input from the students

Simulations

Computer **simulations** allow students to explore the factors that affect many different situations. They can be a powerful tool to stimulate thinking, reasoning and discussion about, for example:

- Experiments
- Historical situations
- Environmental issues
- Economic conditions
- Geographical impact of change

Allowing students to control one element at a time focuses attention on the combination of factors that influence the outcome.

Computer games

Students play **computer games** all the time out of school and often learn a lot from them – thinking skills, strategy, planning, understanding sequencing, cause and effect as well as literacy, numeracy and mouse and keyboard skills. Many of these skills are useful in school too.

Some of the longer-lived games, such as the group of simulations: **Sim City**, **The Sims** and **Sim Life** (*Electronic Arts*) all offer opportunities to explore scenarios and discuss potential outcomes. Other simulations such as **Age of Empires** (*Microsoft*) achieve the same sort of results. They often rely on the scenario having been set up, which can be quite time consuming, but might appeal to some students in after school clubs.

Computer games

Roller Coaster Tycoon (*Atari*) can be an interesting way of exploring some of the ideas behind economics, budgeting and resource management – useful life skills, but also loosely linked to geography.

When exploring the purpose and value of databases **Championship Manager** (*SIgames*) is a fantastic database with wide appeal.

One of the most valuable uses of games such as these, though, can be to stimulate conversation and team building. Do try them out yourself, or at least have some young expert explain them to you!

Drill and practice activities

Computers can be a great way of **reinforcing** learning. Most children are much happier answering spelling and number tasks on screen, which are then marked by the computer, than they are working through the same tasks with pencil and paper.

A good drill and practice program will:

- Have banks of questions all at the same level
- Allow you to choose the level of questions you want the children to answer
- Give the children meaningful feedback
- Use the timing facility of the computer to add to motivation
- Record children's scores in a way that you can easily access

Resources for revision

There are lots of ICT-based **resources** available on CD-ROM for students'
revision, both for SATs at key stages 2 and 3 and also for GCSE and A-level. Many of
them offer immediate marking and annotated answers which help students
understand where they need to improve or have gone wrong.

Revision resources are best at:

- Testing knowledge of facts
- Providing lots of example questions
- Giving children confidence

Make sure students understand that revision resources:

- Must follow an appropriate curriculum
- May not cover all the different question types they'll get in the exam
- May not ask them to write their answers, and that they'll need to practise this too.

Software tools

Software tools are the pieces of software that allow us to do things. Word processors, art packages, spreadsheets and databases all fall into this category. Most children will have access to office-standard programs on their computers at home. There are, however, many software tools specially designed for younger children and which introduce their full functionality gradually. Choosing which tool to use should be a whole-school decision.

A simpler form of a program is especially valuable for databases and spreadsheets, where visual presentation of the output is important. Some word-processors offer a useful speech facility which reads the children's writing back to them.

Learning to use software tools is best done in a context, so it's important to plan lessons which demand the ICT skills you are trying to teach rather than teaching the skill in isolation.

Subject-specific tools

Subject-specific tools are tools designed with a particular subject or class of subject in mind. A set of tools which could be used by maths may be unsuited to science, for instance. It is important to find tools which you are confident will support your subject teaching.

Factors to take into account when selecting a tool:

- How much time will it take you to teach students to use it?
- Where does it fit in the curriculum?
- Is it a tool that you can use for whole-class teaching?
- Does the tool behave like others the students are using and so build on the skills they already have?

Assessment software

Assessment software can be split into two categories: software that provides **informal** assessment and software that offers **formal** assessment. Make sure the students are not able to alter the level or score that they achieve by any unfair means. Ensuring that scores and results are saved on a secure part of the school server will be important.

Informal assessment software
You can use the games, tests and exercises from websites or software as part of your general assessment programme.

Formal assessment software
This demands more time and more serious involvement from both teachers and students. For grades that are in any way 'official', special assessment software will be the only choice for the teacher. This is a new development currently under consideration by government and examination bodies.

Notes

Introduction

 ICT Equipment

 Choosing & Using Software

 ICT for Class Teaching ◀

 ICT for Learning

 The Internet

 ICT at Home

 Inclusion

ICT for Class Teaching

Getting started

ICT is not a distinct method of teaching – it is a set of tools to aid teaching.
Fit ICT around your lesson plans and your class's needs, not vice versa.

Some considerations when planning ICT use:

- Make an **inventory** of all the equipment at your disposal (both ICT and
  conventional) before you begin planning a lesson

- If you haven't used a piece of ICT equipment before, spend a few minutes with
  someone who has and see what it can do. It may turn out to offer just what you
  are looking for

- One of the features of ICT is that it **bridges physical distance** very well. Think
  about setting up an email or video-conference project with another school – it
  could be in the same town or in New Zealand!

- Look for applications that **excite** you personally. That way your enthusiasm is likely
  to become infectious

Dedicated whole-class lesson

With as high a student/computer ratio as possible, the lesson can be dedicated to using software suitable for your subject or looking at internet/digital resources.

- Make sure that the lesson fits into a sequence of lessons building on children's skills
- Consider providing data-files that the children can manipulate rather than having to type text in from scratch
- Make sure the children know what they have to do – sequential instructions will help
- Use wall space in a dedicated ICT area to provide information that children will need to refer to
- If children are sharing the computer, make sure the rules about taking turns and working together are well understood
- Make sure children know where to save their work. If working in pairs, save it where they can both find it

Group work with ICT resources

A group project
After discussing a shared project, students can use a range of ICT resources with different students carrying out different tasks. One group could be given a digital camera, another access to a computer and printer to edit the images, and another a word-processor and presentation software to arrange a series of slides on the subject.

Sharing a computer for a discussion
With data-logging equipment, for example, a group can use a computer as a focus for the investigation.

- Set rules, eg **all** group members should be **asked their opinions** before making changes on the computer
- Encourage children to **record** what they have discussed as well as the decisions they make
- Make clear what the **plenary session** at the end of the lesson will demand

Ideas for whole-class presentation

Introducing a lesson:
Begin with a **discussion** using an element of a CD-ROM or website via a digital projector or an interactive whiteboard.
Alternatively, a **PowerPoint** presentation with animations, graphics and sounds as well as words is a stimulating opening.

During a lesson:
Consider whether students can be asked to prepare a **presentation** to deliver to classmates in a subsequent lesson.
If students use part of a published program, this helps model the way they will work on the same piece of software on their own.
Involving children in choosing answers from the front of the class adds interest and motivates.

Ending a lesson:
End a lesson with a **plenary**, or view work carried out by members of the class.
Talking through a **worksheet** displayed at the front might be a way of reinforcing the lesson content.

Interactive whiteboards

An interactive whiteboard is a large computer screen, a digital projector and a traditional whiteboard all rolled into one. Teachers and students can write on the board when it is displaying digital content, adding annotations, diagrams or text. Many applications also convert any text handwritten on to the board into typeface and can save work at each step along the way. As well as acting like a normal whiteboard, it can be used in other ways:

Wordfiles	Texts can be highlighted and edited according to objectives
Databases	Can be interrogated as a class activity
Spreadsheets	Data can be entered and analysed by the whole class
Images	Can be annotated to identify main features
Digital films and animations	Can be viewed by whole class for discussion
Websites	Can be visited as on a computer screen
CD-ROMs	Features can be explored and interactions modelled

Interactive whiteboards are very popular in ICT suites, where they can be used to model good ICT practice.

Data projectors

Data Projectors combine the functions of a large film projector and an overhead projector. The device enlarges and projects any image you would be able to view on a computer screen. Although students can't actually draw on the projections, they can enter text or images as normal from any computer the projector is connected to.

Advantages
- Wonderfully portable, so can be shared between a number of classrooms in schools
- Not confined to ICT suite or specific classrooms. Can be used anywhere with a white wall
- Prepared lessons can be delivered and shared by everyone

Disadvantages
- There is a small amount of set-up time involved with digital projectors. They have to be given a suitable position and be at a correct angle to the surface they are projecting on to
- The teacher cannot write directly on the surface they are projecting on to
- Shadows can obstruct students' views if others stand up

Using equipment to prepare teaching presentations

ICT equipment can be used to present:

* PowerPoint slide-type presentations
* Presentations including animations, video, links to web pages etc.
* Skill instructions about how to carry out a task on a computer

Do's and Dont's

✓ Do ask other teachers how they use ICT in their lessons and share ideas and experience

✓ Do make sure that all students can see properly and understand what you are doing – that way they pick up ICT skills as well as the subject you are teaching

✓ Do make sure the internet is available from the location you are going to use

✗ Don't rely only on the technology to run your lesson. Planning is just as important

✗ Don't panic if it does not go to plan. It doesn't matter if your computer crashes once – your students are still likely to be much more engaged than by a textbook-orientated lesson

Using software to prepare teaching presentations

Professional presentation packages allow you to pace your presentation. The keywords and concise definitions that appear on the screen also make ideal notes for students. Use the preset animation feature to build up words on screen – French vocabulary and the English equivalents, for example.

Word processors allow you to write and edit the script of any talk you wish to give.

Database and spreadsheet packages give you the opportunity to create your own store of data from which you can easily create graphs and pie-charts. This might be useful in geography to present climate statistics, for instance.

Using software to prepare teaching presentations

Games can be downloaded from teaching websites, bought individually or come as part of a larger software package. Ideally, they will reinforce what you are trying to teach in an interesting and interactive way. Games might be used in maths to check young children's number bonds, or to explore a scientific concept, such as photosynthesis, or a chemical formula.

Remember:

- Get familiar with the software. Find out what happens if someone presses the wrong key – your students are certain to do so!

- Have a back-up lesson prepared in case something goes wrong – computers sometimes do

- If you are demonstrating, remember to take it slowly. It may take two or three demos before everybody can follow you

Timing factors

The **time** you put into preparing your ICT presentation will be given back to you manifold by the time you save during your lesson. Forget scribbled bits of paper and dodgy enlargements; the smooth transition between examples means that you will be able to stick to the time plan.

Setting-up time for data projectors, computers and software should be allowed before the start of the lesson. Attempting to install a piece of software or download a game halfway through a lesson will bore the students and frustrate you, so prepare in advance!

Remember to factor in time for students to ask a lot of questions. The increased level of interactivity means they may feel more animated than usual.

When using ICT you will find it more difficult to digress far from your original lesson plan as time, software and hardware restrictions usually point you towards your core plan. Despite this, always have activities lasting five, fifteen and thirty minutes on hand to cover an emergency.

Notes

ICT for Learning

Code of practice for ICT use

Your school should have a special **code of practice** for the use of ICT. This should contain details of:

- Any special screening software or 'firewalls' you have in place
- When children are permitted to use the computer and how they will be supervised
- Software licence restrictions
- How much freedom students are given in saving their work – policies about whether the materials are backed up, and whose responsibility that is
- Expectations regarding tidiness in the computer suite
- Expectations regarding whether machines should be turned off or left on standby
- Rules regarding the printing out of material, eg limits on the number of pages, or whether they are colour or black-and-white
- Rules concerning the use of personal email

A version of this should be made available to parents/carers. Teachers and students should understand their responsibilities regarding the code.
For additional considerations relating specifically to the internet see pages 84 & 85.

Co-ordinating ICT within school

ICT co-ordinators within schools should work with other teachers to formulate a general **ICT policy and framework** for all subjects. Each teacher must be clear in their own mind about:

- How much ICT they can realistically put to good use in their lessons
- Where ICT can make a particular contribution to their subject
- Any additional training they need in those ICT skills
- What hardware and software the school has and what they have access to
- What the process is for reviewing and purchasing subject-specific software
- Any procedure to follow before using equipment (eg: locating keys for the computer suite, acquiring any additional passwords they may need, signing out digital cameras, data projectors etc.)

Co-ordinating ICT use and communicating policy is especially important for members of staff who may be under-trained in ICT or who may regard ICT as unhelpful in the teaching of their subject.

ICT skills for children

ICT skills cover a range of activities from using a telephone to building a website, and account for a considerable part of the everyday life of most adults.

Children's ICT skills quickly snowball from the basics that you will teach them. As they use more ICT, whether it's mobile phones, game consoles or educational software, they learn as their need arises. There is no magic order to learning the skills.

Part of the ability to understand and **de-code** information we are given depends on our **understanding** of the medium. Getting to grips with the vast amount of information on the internet is invaluable but it depends on literacy and other skills as much as ICT.

We all need to feel confident when using ICT. For very small children it may start with how to operate a video or a telephone and lead to programming websites as children get older.

Note:
It is common for teachers to feel that they know less about ICT than their students. Sometimes this is the case. Use your students' knowledge to help you and other learners.

Skills overview

There are some **basic skills** that most programs require. Check that you and your students can:

- Open a program
- Open a data-file associated with a program
- Save to a chosen location
- Cut and paste
- Amend the style of something – text, spreadsheet etc.
- Use the mouse to control a pen in an art package, a menu, a game
- Send a selection to a printer
- Use an index to search
- Save elements from one application to another

Using text

'But their typing is so slow'

If you cannot justify **typing** sessions in class, then encourage students to copy and paste text from a website or CD-ROM into their word processor. They can then use the text in a number of ways:

- Find and replace names to change the story
- Add adjectives to make the text more interesting
- Add adverbs to explain the actions
- Change nouns to alter the meaning completely
- Change the order of sentences to amend the story

These different activities encourage students to focus on text and whatever aspect of literacy you want to explore without depending on typing skills. Various software solutions offer text in outline to facilitate these activities, but many factual accounts can be used as starting points. Encourage children to **draft** and **plan** using the computer. They can then use the text they've already typed in to contribute towards their story.

Exploring numbers

Type of software	Pros	Cons
Drill and practice	Presents lots of sums quickly. Timing constraints can make mastery fun	Programs are not always well structured. Trial and error sometimes achieves results
Spreadsheet	Allows time to be spent on analysis, not calculations. Presents graphs quickly	Can produce nonsense if the functions are not understood
Graphing package	Allows time to be spent understanding the graphs	Neat graphs can be produced without real understanding
Shape and space	Allows students to explore shape and understand transformations	Programs sometimes move through the topic too quickly and students can arrive at the right answers without real understanding

Sounds and pictures

Most teenagers will be adept with **MP3 files** of their favourite bands, but not familiar with using sounds in their work at school. Various software exists that enables them to add sounds and to edit presentations they make. Increasingly **libraries of sounds** are available on disc and online.

Children enjoy illustrating their work. **Pictures** can also be used effectively to stimulate writing. It is very easy to incorporate digital images into the work you create on the computer. Many galleries and museums offer **libraries of online searchable pictures** which link directly to National Curriculum topics.

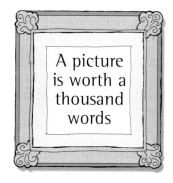

A picture is worth a thousand words

REMEMBER copyright. Encourage children to acknowledge the source of their images.

Control and data-logging

Control projects take outputs from the computer to control bulbs, buzzers and motors. Inputs, meanwhile, are produced by sensors or switches, which affect the lights, buzzers and motors in certain circumstances.

Expensive equipment makes it difficult to facilitate whole class provision, so control projects are generally used by small groups of children. Software mimics can support this subject by simulating the effects of real inputs and outputs just using the computer.

Data-logging fits into the geography curriculum when exploring weather, for instance, or in science for monitoring temperature change in exercising humans.

Limited equipment usually restricts data-logging to group work. You need to plan in plenty of time for analysis of the data captured and the graphs produced.

Multimedia creation

Multimedia creation takes time in the classroom, but can be immensely motivating and exciting for those taking part. Make sure you have an appropriate tool to use. Projects that work especially well include history topics, where the pictorial resources add to the text information provided, or local geography or science projects where students can explain the local area or the topic to others.

It is easier if the information does not have to be created sequentially, though there have been some exciting resources made by children telling stories illustrated with pictures, sounds and music.

Multimedia creation

Steps in a multimedia project

Scoping a project

Agreeing on the content

Choosing the platform

Selecting the media and techniques: the treatment

Interface design

The writing team

Audio asset production

Video asset production

Graphics asset production

Putting it all together

Testing

Assessment

Considerations

Make sure the team knows who the audience is

Make sure the team knows the scope of the project and is not too ambitious (especially the first time)

Select a team that is balanced between those with ideas, and those who work hard

Spend time planning the roles of the team so everyone knows who has to do what

Spend a lot of time planning before the writing and designing starts

Make sure there is a real audience and that outsiders can enjoy the end result – headteacher, governors and parents are usually positive audiences

The graphics tablet

A **graphics tablet** links to a computer and is operated with a stylus or pen. It relies on software to translate the position of the pen on the tablet into the position of the cursor on the computer screen. It allows students to use art packages with a pen rather than a mouse, thus enabling a greater degree of artistic control.

You will need to buy an art package too. Some art packages specifically support graphics tablets. Some, for instance, support pressure sensitivity, which controls boldness and width of lines on screen. This can be a real advantage if you want to achieve different effects.

Think about what size of tablet best suits your needs – a range of sizes is available. You'll also need to come up with a strategy for making sure you keep all the pens!

Locating computers for independent study

There are a number of options when considering where to place computers which will be used for teaching purposes. Schools often allow students access to computers before or after school or at lunch-time, and other considerations may need to be taken into account.

Issues to consider:

- Are there any limitations as to where students can log on to the network and still access their work?

- Is it important that there is an adult present when students are using the computers?

- Can computers in the library be available outside lesson hours?

- When can maintenance be carried out if the suites and continued access to them are to be supported?

- How can you ensure that the computer is a food and drink free zone?

- How will you ensure that students are not given unsupervised access to either the internet or teachers' files?

How long do you need?

Deciding how much time you need on the computer is sometimes a matter of circumstance. If you are timetabled for the suite then you will probably wish to plan to use the computers for the whole lesson.

- **Setting-up** and **demonstration** time have to be considered if you are planning to use ICT for whole-class teaching

- It is very frustrating for students if you give them **too short** a time to get into a piece of work on the computer before you move on. Twenty minutes should be the minimum time available. Older children will work on a computer productively for significantly longer

- Make sure children **save** their work regularly

- Make sure there is enough time at the end of the lesson to discuss what has been achieved, and **if necessary** to print out work completed

- Children who take a **long time** to type text in could be given help either by a classroom assistant or by a more keyboard-skilful colleague; alternatively prepare text in advance if the purpose of the exercise is not developing keyboard skills

- Encourage children to **share** expertise and shortcuts

Assessment issues

ICT can help make the **assessment** process less laborious for both student and teacher. Most subject-specific software and websites will come with games and tests that can store the progress that students make. This is particularly valuable for testing knowledge and facts.

Remember:

- A history test on a computer should not require amazing ICT skills to complete – then you would be testing ICT not history

- A test designed to explore ICT skills should be just that – perhaps a task to create a document, a graph etc. Saving results at different stages of the process will give a clear indication of students' skills. Observation of how students go about the task will teach you a lot about their knowledge and understanding

- Make use of the fact that the test is on a computer – don't just use the same type of test you would set on paper. Use the medium to make the test seem more exciting and interactive

Notes

Introduction

 ICT Equipment

 Choosing & Using Software

 ICT for Class Teaching

 ICT for Learning

 The Internet ◀

 ICT at Home

 Inclusion

The Internet

Code of practice for internet safety

The school

Your school should have a special **code of practice** for use of the internet. It should outline both what the school's policies are and what the student must agree to.

What the school can do:

- Provide details of any special screening software or 'firewalls' that are in place
- Write a disclaimer stating that neither the school nor the Internet Service Provider (ISP) can guarantee 100% safety from inappropriate materials
- Give details of when children are permitted to use the internet and how they will be supervised
- Say whether or not the sites visited during lessons are pre-selected by teachers
- Specify how much freedom students are given when conducting their own research on the web
- Offer a reminder that a log is kept of all sites visited by each user

Code of practice for internet safety

The student

What the student should agree to do:

- Pledge that the internet will only be used for school work, unless permission is given
- Acknowledge the source of all downloaded materials
- Pledge not to deliberately access unsuitable material, and agree that should any be found accidentally, procedures for reporting this will be followed
- Be aware of sanctions for breaches of the agreed policy (ultimately, dismissal for staff, exclusion for students and withdrawal of access for community users)
- Accept that the possession of certain types of unsuitable material can lead to prosecution by the police

A version of this should be made available to parents/carers. Teachers and students should understand their responsibilities regarding this code.

Safety

Content

The world wide web is largely an **uncensored zone**. Special settings on most search engines allow you to filter adult content from search results. It is not just pornography that might cause you problems in school. Other information and images that students can find on the web may prove just as undesirable – downloading instructions to make a pipe-bomb, or racist jokes, for example.

The safest way of using the internet with children is to give them specific web addresses with sites that you want them to use. This may be especially appropriate for young children. At home and out of school, though, they will be using search engines for themselves; teaching them to surf safely is an important part of learning to use the internet.

Show them how to use sites which provide links to places they might want – www.bbc.co.uk is a good and secure starting point.

Safety

Communicating with people

The internet offers a range of ways of **communicating** with other people, some of which are more risky than others.

Email allows you to communicate directly with people who have your address. If you **leave your email address** or personal details on message boards or join chat rooms, then unknown people will have access to it.

Message boards are a good place to read others' thoughts and comments about issues of shared interest. Many ask you to log on and you can only reply to the board, not to contributors. Generally people do not moderate what is said here and messages may be infrequent.

Safety

Communicating with people

A **chat room** is a space where a number of people online at the same time can all talk together. Students wouldn't want to read out their telephone number or personal details in a crowded coffee shop; announcing them in a chat room to a stranger is no different.

Students should be aware that the 16-year-old girl they have been getting on well with, and have arranged to meet might just be a 40-year-old man. **It may not be necessary to teach students to avoid internet discussions; it is necessary to teach them to exercise caution.**

Expectations

If you don't use the right keywords or if you look in the wrong places, you could search the internet for hours without finding anything useful to you.

If you are not prepared for the time and effort involved in sorting through links, then the internet can seem like a very confusing waste of time.

By spending just a few minutes explaining what students can expect from the internet – the frustrations as well as the joys – you can prevent:

- Time-wasting when they are looking for resources
- Disillusionment if they fail to find anything
- A barrage of questions from students when they are searching
- Students deliberately searching for material that is not relevant

It's worth remembering that for the students you are only one source of information about the internet. Others include family members, friends, magazines, TV, radio etc.

Using the internet with students

A good way to introduce students to the internet is to set them a **resource-finding test**. Here's how to do it:

1. Find a number of resources with a connected theme. It is important that they range from the highly interactive to the purely informative.
2. Create an activity around these sites that supports a worksheet with gaps left for answers students can only find by getting information from the sites.
3. Make sure there is not too much work for your students to finish during the lesson time.
4. Help those who lack confidence with the internet, and remember to encourage and set further tasks for those who are finding the exercise too easy.

Helping students find relevant information

Filling in gaps is a popular exercise for helping students to capture information, but **other** things they might do include storing pictures captured from the internet to add into a database record card they create, or making tables of information – names, sizes, weights, food preferences of different animals, for instance.

General tips and guidance:

- Make sure that children are aware that not all the information they read on the internet is **true** or lacking in **bias**
- Make sure children know how to find out **when** the information was put online. That might make a difference to its accuracy or relevance
- Encourage children to check findings on **more than one site** to see if the information is the same. The populations of different countries is an interesting topic to explore in this respect
- Guide children towards exploring some environmental lobbying sites to illustrate the sort of language that might be used **to persuade** rather than present facts

Top tips for internet success

To help children find information on the internet:

- Make sure they have been trained to conduct a detailed search
- If they are too young to search, give them precise addresses
- Know your websites as well as you would know a book or video you were using with your class
- Check that the websites you are recommending link only to relevant sites
- If it's some time since you created your website list, check that the links still work – websites change quite often!
- Carefully plan the activities you want the children to do at the website
- Monitor the children and make sure they are on task
- Pin up a list of addresses of the major online encyclopaedias and resource sites in the computer room and allow a space for students to recommend their own favourite sites

Searching for internet resources

Learn to **adapt your search** depending on the type of resources you wish to find:

- Use an '**advanced search**' function to eliminate specific, non-relevant results that keep reappearing

- Some **search engines** give prominent places to sites that pay to advertise; many are unlikely to list small or non-commercial sites. Try to find out what kinds of sites each engine tends to choose and select your engine accordingly

- Sites do not have to be big to be useful. Many school sites act as portals to a host of tried-and-tested resources

- Try varying your **keywords**. If you are searching for illustrations of Roman clothing, try combinations such as 'Roman fashion', 'ancient clothing', 'ancient Roman garments' etc.

Small websites

- Remember not to overlook **smaller websites**. Many schools have their own sites which are run by enthusiastic teachers and offer excellent resources for free

- **Museums**, non-commercial organisations and **charities** can be a great source of free resources for teaching

- **Bookmark** the exact page you want children to visit using 'Favourites' on your web-browser. For example, **www.ancientegypt.co.uk/pyramids/home.html** takes you to the page about the pyramids specifically, not the home page for the Ancient Egypt site

- Decide **what type of resources** you want for a particular lesson and search for each one separately. If you want an excellent online tutorial and a brilliant game, you may have to look in two different places. Don't be afraid of ending up with a host of links for different aspects of the lesson – that accurately mirrors normal internet research

- **Create a list of detailed web addresses** as a file that you save to the computer network. Children can click on it or copy it into their browser to access the exact parts of the sites you have directed them to

Internet resources for teachers

The internet is probably the most exciting reference tool ever created. Visiting **www.teachernet.gov.uk.** for example, will provide you with information about current teaching practice; you can find information about the National Curriculum at the QCA site, **www.qca.org.uk**, while sites such as **inclusion.ngfl.gov.uk** will tell you about inclusion and about students with particular difficulties.

Internet resources for teachers

Other useful sites include:

Becta www.ictadvice.org.uk Government agency with advice on ICT

BESA www.besanet.org.uk British Educational Suppliers Association. Industry-led site with information about resources

Curriculum online www.curriculumonline.gov.uk Government-run software listing website

DfES www.dfes.gov.uk Department for Education's site with wide range of information about education, as well as ICT

IPAS www.ipas.ngfl.gov.uk Independent ICT Procurement Advisory Service for Schools

National Curriculum Online www.nc.uk.net Links every National Curriculum programme of study requirement to resources

NAACE www.naace.org Organisation for advisors on the use of ICT in the classroom

OFSTED www.ofsted.gov.uk School inspection reports and much more can be found here

Schoolzone www.schoolzone.co.uk Evaluators of software for Curriculum Online

TEEM www.teem.org.uk Classroom-based evaluations of software from UK teachers

Times Educational Supplement www.tes.co.uk Web version of Friday publication

Downloading and creating teaching materials

The internet is not just useful for downloading whole lesson plans. You can also download either specific materials or items which you can modify to create your own course materials. The wonderful thing about the web is that everything from museum homepages to enthusiasts' sites might carry a great diagram or picture for you to illustrate, say, the water cycle, Monet, photosynthesis or even alliteration!

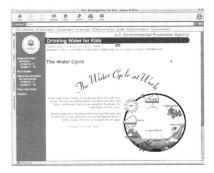

Providing resources for students to use at home

When you are providing electronic resources for students to use you need to consider the practicality of students transporting files between home and school.

- Email is attractive if students have email access
- Bringing floppy discs into school is less reliable and can introduce viruses

Think also about the software that children are likely to have access to at home:

Software	Issues
Browser – most will be using Internet Explorer but may not have the most recent version. **Websites**	Only students with internet access can visit from home, so consider whether children will have access at school out of class time.
Word processor	Most computers will have some sort of word processor, so children can read files, especially those saved in .rtf format.
Acrobat files	If the home user has downloaded the reader from the internet, these can be read and printed out but not edited.

Copyright implications

Copyright issues in schools have become much more openly discussed in the past few years. Many LEAs, for example, have bought the licences to use Ordnance Survey maps for all their schools and so on. A photocopy betrays its origins whereas an electronic copy does not. The internet is still not an effectively regulated electronic library, but that is not a licence to abuse it.

Points to bear in mind:

- Images and text are freely available on the internet but **that does not mean they are copyright free!**
- Most materials can be copied by individual children for the purpose of their education, but **only for their own use**
- If you run a successful school website and have lots of children's work up there alongside images taken from somewhere else on the web you will be **infringing copyright**
- Once you have published to the web you have changed the **status** of the copy
- Children should be directed to **acknowledge** the source of their materials
- If you copy a piece of text, put it in quotes and **acknowledge** the author

Plagiarism

Computers make it very easy to capture chunks of someone else's text, put it into your own document and call it your own. They do, however, offer an interesting solution as well as having compounded the problem:

Copying from one source is plagiarism; copying from two is research.
Wilson Mizner

Where students are asked to create a plan, a first draft, and then to work further on their draft, saving all three elements of the process as separate files, teachers can see completely how the work has developed. Once students are aware that they are being marked in this way, the sudden emergence of a high quality essay downloaded from the internet (or written by mum) should become less likely!

Differentiation

One of the most powerful uses of ICT can be to change and **tailor** resources to suit the needs of particular children.

- Worksheets can have a question added or taken away, amended or enhanced. ICT makes it possible to **differentiate by question** as well as by **outcome**
- Saving a file in several different forms with different levels of difficulty can be a relatively simple task, and ensures that lessons are best suited to the individual needs of the students, both the less and most able
- Some tasks can be presented pictorially or in words
- Resources created on a word processor are easy to edit, but be aware that changing the text can mess up the layout

Communication

The advent of email and the world wide web allows you to **converse** with thousands of teachers and academics up and down the country (and, indeed, in other countries). This allows you freedom to ask their advice on teaching topics or to give them the low down on where to find a particular piece of information.

Equally, children can share their work with others. Projects such as Schoolnet2000 allowed children to publish to the web and share their resources with others. You can also see this in operation at European Schoolnet, www.eun.org

Using email to communicate with other schools and to work jointly on projects is something that depends on setting up email addresses successfully so that classes, or year groups, can access information as it comes in. It can be time-consuming but is usually well worth the effort.

Forming communities

The internet gives you the opportunity to create or join an online **community**.
This could be connected to either teaching, education in your area or a subject of your choice.

Increasingly, software is becoming available that supports communities of students online. Three examples which have been used in the UK education system and which provide student registration and school community management systems are:

- Digital Brain, www.digitalbrain.com
- Think.com, www.think.com
- Ramesys www.ramesys.com/education/

These are secure and inaccessible to uninvited guests. They offer a safe environment in which children can share information and work on projects and tasks together.

Home-school communication

The internet allows various **communication channels** to open up between students' homes and the school.

A school homepage, for instance, may be a constantly updated source of information for parents/carers and students, reminding them of forthcoming topics and events, term dates, school trips and so on.

Home-school communication

Email, similarly, has the potential to greatly improve communication **levels** between home and school.

- For the school-student relationship, it can be a motivational tool to get some students to submit work via email
- For the school-parent relationship, many parents/carers find it a much more acceptable form of communication than the traditional 'letter home' or 'teacher's note' lost with the lunchbox at the bottom of the school bag. The fact that information bypasses the student altogether can allow issues to be dealt with more confidentially and, if need be, without the student's knowledge

However, it is important to be sensitive to the parent community and not exclude those who do NOT have easy access to email. For them, the note in the school bag may still be an important communication route.

Implications for school administration

If email is to be a regular communication medium, it is crucial that the **school administration** is equipped to respond to emails from parents/carers.

Some issues to consider:

- **Who receives** the email from parents/carers at school? The secretary, form teacher, year head, head teacher?
- **What response time** will email get? Same day, three working days, one working week?
- **Will parents/carers be taught** how to use the service, ie not to send off a hasty email at the first sign of an issue, but to temper their comments?
- **Will any check be needed** that the email has actually come from the parent/carer, not a disgruntled student?
- **Will staff be taught** how to respond to parents/carers too?
- **How will emails be recorded?** Some may raise issues that need to go 'on file'

ICT at Home

Continuing learning

61% of students have computers at home, according to the Statistics of Education survey of ICT in 2002.

This means that at the end of the school day many students, have the opportunity to access **more** learning resources. Access to a wide range of web-based resources has revolutionised the homework habits of many students for whom the internet has become the first port of call.

Making sure that students without the facilities at home can access computer rooms after school, or even at breakfast-time, can lead to greater ICT usage, and, more importantly, greater involvement with education. If the local library has a computer or two available, make sure the students know that too.

Building on home use

As well as completing homework and set tasks, students use their computer at home for a wide range of reasons.
Those with internet access may well use:

- Email
- Messaging services where they can talk to friends and family online
- Computer games
- Internet shopping sites
- Community sites – cheats for games, sites about their favourite bands, teams etc.
- Websites that support television programmes

All of these develop skills in typing, searching, planning and thinking, and can reinforce work in school.

Practical lesson extensions

Whatever the subject you teach, a student with internet access outside of school hours should be able to **continue** with their studies where your lesson left off. Not everyone will have a PC or internet access at home, but it is worth remembering that many students will have opportunities to use these facilities at friends' houses, libraries, youth centres, school, etc.

Consider the following:

- Make a **list** of suitable websites, CDs, DVDs, videos and CD-ROMs available to students. The range of hardware needed to operate the recommendations should be as wide as possible to be inclusive

- Try to make the **range** of resources as extensive as possible. (eg recommendations for a topic on the 17th Century should cover everything from the music of the period to its leading philosophers and even gruesome medical experiments!)

- Ask students to talk about what resources they have **enjoyed**, including both the ones you recommended and the ones they found. Make this a regular feature for a few minutes at the end of a class

Homework

Until all children have ICT access out of school, it is difficult to set compulsory tasks that necessarily involve using the internet, a PC or software at home.

ICT-generated homework, however, does not necessarily require any ICT equipment at all on behalf of the student. Try the following examples:

1. Ask the students to come up with their own design for a website about your subject. They can write and draw 'screenshots' of the finished product containing all the aspects of the topic they enjoy.
2. Use a website or software in class that gives students a test. Ask them to come up with their own test along similar lines to try out on a partner the following week.
3. At the start of a new topic ask students to find out anything they can about X. Verification of the facts they discover can come either via whole-class internet activity or discussion.

Giving advice to parents and carers

Many parents/carers ask for **advice** from teachers about what software to buy and how to help their children.

Some principles:

* Sharing computers between children can be effective as children learn to discuss what they are doing
* Locating the computer in a living room or shared space can help parents keep track of what their children are viewing
* Setting up the internet access so that it blocks access to inappropriate sites is important
* Avoid software that claims to suit a wide age range, especially for a specific subject. Few pieces of software will be really suitable for children aged 4 to 12
* Look for software that offers reference information as this is likely to support children's learning best
* Encourage parents to buy software that you do not have in school – there's so much available that the school does not have time to explore
* Above all, remind parents/carers that the computer can be fun. Children learn best when they are laughing!

Inclusion

Supporting children's learning

A PC in the classroom or time in the ICT suite can mean that students of all abilities are given the opportunity to follow up their **own** interests at a level that ideally suits their learning pace.

A child who has a goldfish, for instance, might want to search for information about the species. Try to ensure that all children are given the opportunity and skills to follow their own interests.

There are many websites which support children's particular passions – pop groups, TV shows, sporting interests and so on. These can be great places to start to find text for the reluctant learner. These often engage more effectively than standard texts.

Using specialist hardware

If you have a student who has need for **specialist hardware** to support his or her computer access there are a number of issues to consider:

- Does the equipment need to be available on one computer, or a number of computers?
- Is it fixed or portable?
- Does it require special software and if so where must that be loaded and saved?
- Is it robust, and does it need changing as the student's skills develop?

The government website, inclusion.ngfl.gov.uk includes descriptions of many resources available for children with particular needs at different ages, and for different areas of the curriculum.

Make sure you ask advice from those in your LEA who work regularly with children with particular needs, as they may have experience of different equipment and know the merits of different systems.

Tools to support accessibility

There is a range of **tools** available to support students with particular access issues including those that:

- Read text to blind students
- Read text back as the user types
- Remove the need for keyboard access by entering computer controls through switches

If you have children who require this kind of support, discuss their needs with your school's special educational needs co-ordinator and with staff from the inclusion team at your LEA. Alternatively, visit the inclusion website, given on the previous page, to join one of the forums supporting special interest groups, eg: SENCO forum, special educational needs and ICT, or English as an additional language.

Specialist software

Publishers such as *Inclusive Technology, Wigit and SEMERC* specialise in software specifically designed to support students with special needs.

Do not be tempted to substitute programs designed for much younger children. While these might be at the appropriate level of teaching objective, they are unlikely to stimulate the students. This is especially true of software that includes narrative or illustrations as opposed to photographic resources.

The greatest exception to this is **software tools** – those designed for key stage 1 students may well suit older, less able children. Reference to software in this category can again be found on the government inclusion website, including some case studies describing how the software has been used.

Equal opportunities

When supervising students' ICT use, always keep sight of equal opportunities guidelines by making sure that:

- Each group or individual gets an **equal** amount of time at the computer
- No one child **dominates** the group or hijacks the computer
- No child is **excluded** from the group or denied a proper turn at the computer

Remember also to:

- **Intervene** whenever you feel it will benefit the lesson
- Change the **groupings** if it will benefit the students
- Keep a note of the different **work rates** of single-sex and mixed groups
- Keep control of how **many** students are in each group
- Have at hand a method of generating **random** groups

Confidentiality

Sometimes, searching through computer files, or the huge amount of data on the internet, can reveal material that is confidential or embarrassing to students or teachers.

Internet

When searching for someone's relative on the 1851 census, we may find them classified as an 'imbecile' or an 'idiot' – something that may embarrass the descendant. Yet most of the information that people would prefer not to have divulged is much less obvious. Students or teachers may object to having themselves or their relatives referred to at all, even if it is in a positive context.

Whether you are a geography teacher locating online maps of the area 100 years ago, or a history teacher searching local conscientious objectors, try to make sure that you won't be compromising anybody's confidentiality.

Files

Students must be taught not to open others' files without their permission. Doing so is like going into someone's desk and opening their books. Many students will love the idea of 'locking' people out of their own files and breaking into other people's, so use dramatic analogies and examples to capture their attention.

Removing barriers to learning

Spending time with students in the ICT suite or on a computer in the classroom can remove a number of barriers to learning:

Physical
The world wide web gives you the opportunity to visit thousands of places and read hundreds of books at the touch of a button. Software is available that will allow you to do the kinds of physical tasks which would be otherwise difficult or demanding, such as printing photos, looking at the Mona Lisa in close-up or landing a plane.

Psychological
The internet is a very non-hierarchical way of learning. Many sites are created by peers rather than the usual 'authority figures', so with just a little help students will be able to find a level of learning they feel comfortable with.

Social
Children who may feel that the education system is at odds with the rest of their life often appreciate that the internet gives them the opportunity to learn whilst involved in activities or games they enjoy.

Working with more able students

Computers offer tools and facilities that are an obvious resource to use with more able students. They support individuality well, but at the same time students using them can be included within the mainstream class activity.

- Allowing more able students to **test their abilities** is vital if you want them to stay motivated
- The internet allows students to explore areas **outside** the range and limits of the ordinary curricula, using search engines to pursue special interests
- Website and software tests and activities will allow students to progress to the **highest** level they can
- Students can learn **advanced** skills in even 'simple' software tools, such as word processors and spreadsheets.
- ICT software and hardware can allow gifted or able students new **creative tools**, eg using presentation software for a talk or using a design package for an art project
- Students can **communicate** with others of a similar ability in other schools removing the sense of intellectual isolation

Planning extension activities

Sometimes just expecting more able students to write more deeply and analytically will be enough. But ICT offers opportunities for those with real **creativity** and **skills** in a number of different areas to shine.

- There may be an out-of-school culture of creating a website using HTML among some of the students. Could that be legitimised as a way of publishing a class newspaper or report?

- Can high level writing or thinking skills be turned into planning and organising? Could the able student become the team manager for a larger and longer term project, and be required to present his or her planning to you before the project starts?

- ICT demands many talents from those who are skilful at it. Offering students opportunities to use ICT to demonstrate those talents can be very rewarding for all involved

Allowing time

One of the greatest frustrations for many of us when using ICT is not having enough time: the graph doesn't look quite right, the axis label needs editing, the layout of the leaflet isn't quite centred, the indexing of the document hasn't quite worked.

One of the really valuable characteristics of ICT is that you can edit, amend, refine and represent information or resources without having to start all over again. But it demands **TIME** and it's really important to let students have enough time to create things to their own satisfaction sometimes.

It's easy to think this specifically applies to the most able, but less able students like to be able to get things just right too.

ICT and thinking skills

Knowledge, **comprehension** and **application** are more concrete thinking skills usually developed as part of a formal education. **Analysis**, **synthesis** and **evaluation** require more abstraction and are known as critical thinking skills. ICT can make an active contribution to developing critical thinking skills by:

- Reducing the time spent in plotting graphs, carrying out calculations and simply finding information thereby allowing students more time to **analyse** data

- Providing opportunities for students to bring a variety of evidence together and **synthesise** it into one document, presentation or multimedia object

- Encouraging students to provide feedback to each other, often online, about what they have been doing. This form of **evaluation** is an important part of learning the dialogue of adult life

About the author

Anne Sparrowhawk B.Ed

Anne runs an educational consultancy company, Sparrowhawk and Heald Ltd which has for almost ten years worked in the field of ICT and education. In this context she has worked on many projects involving school research and actively working with resources, teachers and children in school. Motivated by the importance of learning and education, Anne is clear that ICT can make a valuable contribution to that process, but is not driven by the excitement of new technology alone. Stealth learning, when children are fully engaged by the computer task in front of them, can be really exciting and is to be valued. In addition to her consultancy work, Anne was a founding Director of TEEM, a web-based service through which teachers publish classroom-based evaluations of computer programs to help others identify titles best suited to their needs. Anne is based in Cambridge and can be contacted via email at anne@sparrowhawkandheald.co.uk

Pocketbooks

Clear, effective and fast transfer of learning is central to the Pocketbooks' approach. Sold worldwide and published in numerous languages, Pocketbooks have built a loyal following over some two decades. Now there is the Teachers' Series.

Order Form

Your details

Name _____

Position _____

School _____

Address _____

_____

_____

Telephone _____

Fax _____

E-mail _____

VAT No. (EC only) _____

Your Order Ref

Please send me:

No.
copies

ICT in the Classroom _____ Pocketbook ☐

_____ Pocketbook ☐

_____ Pocketbook ☐

_____ Pocketbook ☐

_____ Pocketbook ☐

Order by Post

Teachers'
Pocketbooks

Laurel House, Station Approach
Alresford, Hants. SO24 9JH UK

Order by Phone, Fax or Internet

Telephone: +44 (0)1962 735573
Facsimile: +44 (0)1962 733637
E-mail: sales@teacherspocketbooks.co.uk
Web: www.teacherspocketbooks.co.uk

The series includes:

The Teachers' Pocketbooks Series